MY CAT IS A DICK

MY CAT IS A DICK

Malcolm Katz

First published in Great Britain in 2016 by Trapeze
an imprint of The Orion Publishing Group Ltd
Carmelite House, 50 Victoria Embankment
London EC4Y 0DZ

An Hachette UK Company

10 9 8 7 6 5 4

Copyright © Orion Publishing Group Ltd 2016

Edited by Holly Harley
Designed by Briony Hartley

A CIP catalogue record for this book is
available from the British Library.

ISBN: 978 1 409 16902 4

Printed in Italy

www.orionbooks.co.uk

HELPS OUT AROUND THE HOUSE

DELICIOUS HYDRATION!

Find somewhere else to
wash your hands.

I'll take as much time
as I need, thanks.

Where does this waterfall go...?

- Do you think this bath might've been for someone else?
- Nah.

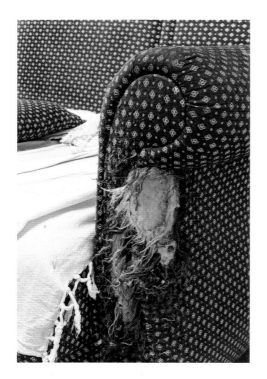

Haven't you heard
of 'shabby chic'?

Just hanging out.

I'M JUST STRETCHING, NO CLAWS. PROMISE.

It's important to make sure your plants are pruned properly.

I knew these flowers were really for me.

Ugh, where are you going? You don't need whatever's in here.

Nope, not for clothes, this is for me.

You don't need to pack any more.

What? It's warm in here.

Mmm, yes, really
lemony fresh.

LAP IT UP.

I've had enough of your rudeness about 'hygiene'.

How else am I
supposed to keep
cool with all this fur?

Try and stop me.

I'm helping.

WHERE ARE THE TREATS?!

I'm done helping.

Just wait till I tread this ash into your carpet.

Why can't you just turn the heating on?

AVOIDS THE LIMELIGHT

Tickle me or go away.

My jams are better
than your jams.

Whatever you were
looking at is far less
important than me.

YOU CAN LOCK ME UP BUT
YOU CAN'T STOP ME.

Don't be mad about
how much better than
you I look.

If I could flip you the bird, that's what I'd be doing right now.

I'm going to spend all of this on catnip.

ALRIGHT, DARLING?!

PLAYS WELL WITH OTHERS

Back off, puny human.

Easy like Sunday morning.

What's in here?
Can I eat it?

You'll never finish
this anyway.

GET AWAY FROM ME
WITH THAT THING.

Makeitstopmakeitstopmakeitstopppppp!

I don't care if you disapprove of my mentoring scheme.

If this makes me
sick later I'll definitely
blame the dog.

STOP FOLLOWING ME.

You expect me to get along with this vegan weirdo?

I tire of these childish games.

GENEROUS SPIRIT

It's always a struggle to
find the perfect present.

Woah, OK, you don't need
to overreact like that.
I'm just being thoughtful!

I'm at a loss to be honest.
Mouse is a classic.
How could you not like it?

This festive cheer is exhausting...

...there's not even anything edible.

Deck the floors.

THIS IS MY TREE NOW.

Here's your weekly allowance after my allocation for treats.

Where are my gifts?!

TRICK OR TREAT?
TREAT. ALL THE TREATS.

Every party needs a pooper.

STRONG WORK ETHIC

Yeah, in a minute.

It's important to make sure I'm properly limber before a hard day of lolling about.

Your filing system needs serious work.

Great bed, thanks. Can't wait to leave bits of it all over the house.

YOUR NOTES ARE SO BORING

Come on, I'm so small
you can still use nearly
all of the keyboard!

Hopefully these papers will fall off the desk so I can play with them.

'Let me put you on hold' - I mean, ignore you and keep watching TV.

I know you told me not to but a little help please?!

Engines purr, I purr, I don't really see what the problem is here.

Why are you looking at me like I will be any help at all? I think I might even be stuck.

You have so many other books, why do you need this one?

I'm just waiting until she looks up and then I'll start kneading this. Claws out and all.

Colouring is boring. You know what's not boring? Food. Feed me.

YOUR MIXING SUCKS.
LET ME TAKE OVER.

LOVES THE GREAT OUTDOORS

THAT PICNIC BASKET BETTER
HAVE HAM IN IT.

I can't wait to throw this up all over your sofa.

This probably
won't end well.

Hello my fishy friend. You look delicious.

Not sure where to go from here, actually. Help?

IT'S DRIZZLING!
LET ME IN!

I am not lifting a single paw while this monstrosity is attached to my body.

SOMEONE SCRATCHED
YOUR PAINTWORK.

This is great for birdwatching but let's just speed up the inevitable and warn the fire brigade now.

So, where in the house do you want these?

Who is that in the garden?! I'm going to have to yowl all night to warn them off.

Out of my way, fatty.

Ugh, going through there looks so tiresome. Open the door.

RESPECTS
BOUNDARIES

Your sofa is vomitrocious.

This bed is lovely and soft. Shame it's so wriggly.

I love this climbing frame!

LET ME SEE THE BIRDS.

THAT SMELLS GOOD.

That smells good too.

I'm almost certain I won't like this but quality control is important to me.

This is a fine drinking vessel, thanks.

YES PLEASE.

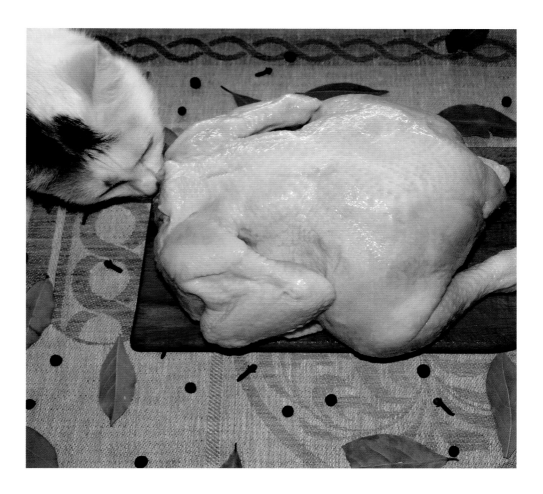

You'd get salmonella eating it like this anyway.

Swim into my belly, boxed fish.

We need to have a serious talk about your internet history.

I need to keep my mind sharp for future schemes.

I'm sick of these toys.

CREDITS

ikurdymov/shutterstock

Exclusive Visual/iStock

sdominick/iStock

David Elfstrom/iStock

Yegor Larin/shutterstock

Lulamej/iStock

vvvita/iStock

Chang Ching Hwong/iStock

simonidadjordjevic/iStock

Michelle Gibson/iStock

Tammy Fullum/iStock

blueperfect/iStock

stenli88/iStock

MelissaMorphew/iStock

JCImagen/iStock

Kateryna Yakolieva/
shutterstock

Lulamej/iStock

koldunova/iStock

Ysbrand Cosijn/iStock

Ysbrand Cosijn/iStock

karamysh/shutterstock

tuggboat/iStock

juffy/iStock

kuban_girl/iStock

robyvannucci/iStock

mile84/iStock

Dashabelozerova/iStock

Bradley Hebdon/iStock

lvalue
http://bit.ly/1WQviZf*

Valerio Pardi/shutterstock

Sementinov/iStock

Smokey Joe
Anna Valentine

Max
Judy Gee

DanBrandenburg/iStock

shyflygirl/iStock

Jennifer Oehler/iStock

alexmak72427/iStock

lissart/iStock

piccerella/iStock

DRB Images, LLC/iStock

Firsilar
Helena Jacoba
http://bit.ly/29hK7C5*

Aurora
Adele Pullarp

shyflygirl/iStock

eZeePics Studio/iStock

Tyson Paul/iStock

Irina Kozorog/shutterstock

tzahiV/iStock

sdominick/iStock

hagit berkovich/
shutterstock

lisa mory/iStock

Commodore Gandalf
Cunningham
http://bit.ly/1UOxiYN*

RoniMeshulamAbramovitz/
iStock

Daniel Hjalmarson/
shutterstock

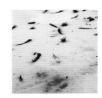
David Claassen/iStock

rosiegirl14/iStock

Redzaal/iStock

ikurdymov/shutterstock

ikurdymov/shutterstock

Tibanna79/shutterstock

Crissy1982/iStock

YURY KISIALIOU/iStock

T_A_Hammonds/iStock

ArtMarie/iStock

Lovelywalk/iStock

rollover/iStock

NOISO PHOTOGRAPHY/
shutterstock

kimeveruss/iStock

ArtyAlison/iStock

eZeePics Studio/iStock

ksushsh/iStock

ksushsh/iStock

Creative Lab/shutterstock

Agnes Kantaruk/
shutterstock

alexmak72427/iStock

Exclusive Visual/iStock

TETE3138/iStock

silkenphotography/iStock

Astrid Gast/iStock

mile84/iStock

Fabio Iamanna/iStock

danchooalex/iStock

AlenaPaulus/iStock

tzahiV/iStock

gldburger/iStock

Waltraud Ingerl/iStock

Ricardo De Mattos/iStock

Philip
Hugh Tanton

images72/Shutterstock

Serenethos/iStock

tirc83/iStock

fotokate/iStock

Kemter/iStock

mishanik_210/shutterstock

donald_gruener/iStock

Astrid Gast/iStock

stephanieanjo/iStock

Tony Campbell/
shutterstock

lofilo/iStock

Janice Waltzer
http://bit.ly/1THf8Ry*

Cate Frost/Shutterstock

Herbert
Natasha Vouckelatou

Herbert
Natasha Vouckelatou

Carlos Castro
http://bit.ly/1WpGLy*

mhobl: http://bit.ly/1XWfljC*

Benjamin Gelman/iStock

ToskanaINC/shutterstock

Gnat
Jane Hughes

Aurora
Adele Pullarp

oversnap/iStock

Valentina Azhgirevich/
iStock

kuban_girl/iStock

Audrey Roorda/iStock

Justin Dolske
http://bit.ly/1pZLDN5*

Cookie
Dean Brindle
http://bit.ly/1NS3Do5*

Jane Hughes